IKIGAI
What makes your life worthwhile?

© Alta H Haffner 2024
ALL RIGHTS RESERVED

ISBN: 978-0-7961-6661-6 (print)

978-0-7961-6662-3 (e-book)

alta@sakurabookpublishing.com

sakurabookpublishing.com

IKIGAI

Ikigai: "iki" means "to live," and "gai" means "reason," which simply means "a reason to live"… with purpose and joyfully so.

I have been meaning to write this book for about 5 years, a burning desire to share my passion, my purpose.

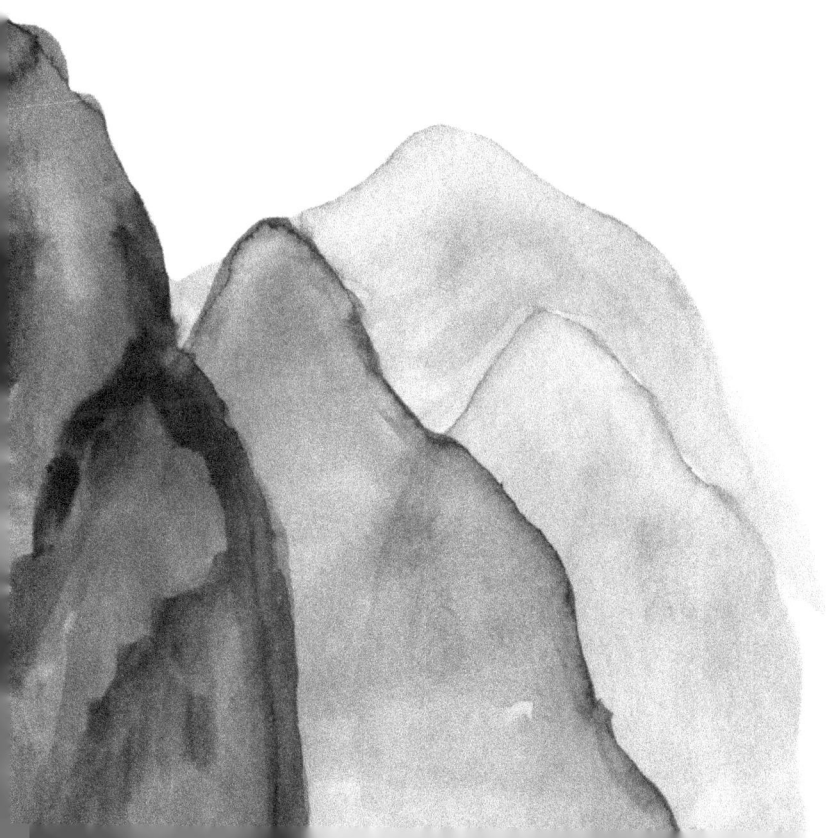

About the Author

Alta H. Haffner is a Haiku po[et] whose work captures the essence [of] precious, fleeting moments w[ith] simplicity and depth. Born with [a] deep appreciation for the beauty [of] brevity, Alta's Haiku poems refle[ct] her keen observation of nature a[nd] her ability to evoke emotions in ju[st] a few short line[s.] Drawing inspiration from the ev[er-]changing seasons, the delica[te] balance of the natural world, a[nd] the quiet whispers of every ne[w] dawn, Alta's Haiku poems invi[te] readers to slow down, pause, a[nd] appreciate the present moment. Wi[th] a handful of syllables, she allo[ws] her readers to contemplate [...] Through her Haiku poetry, Alta Haffner reminds us of the beau[ty] that can be found in simplicity, t[he] power of mindfulness, and t[he] importance of being fully present [in] each moment

We have all done a day's work that left us unfulfilled and unhappy and our souls in a pit of regret.

Every day presents a new opportunity to pursue what sets our hearts on fire. It's never too late to seek the path that brings us joy and fulfillment. Days filled with purpose and passion will feed our souls with contentment. Embrace each moment as a chance to create a richly meaningful life.

wistful longing
escaping to the unknown
memories linger

In those quiet moments of self-reflection, it is natural to feel a longing for the presence of those we can no longer hold close to us. Cherished memories and the warmth of past connections often make us weep.

Though physically apart, the bonds we share with loved ones remain eternally woven into the core of our being, offering comfort and strength in times of solitude. Embracing these memories with gratitude, we will find solace in knowing that love transcends distance and time, continuing to nourish our souls even when we are no longer together in person.

handing out my heart
daily commitment
even when it breaks my heart

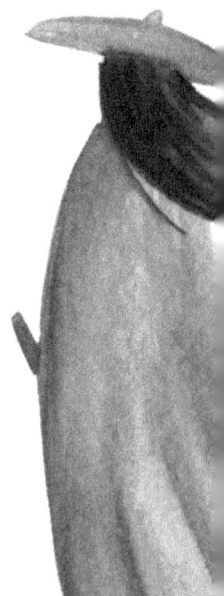

I hand out my heart daily, often when I am not even able to give any part of myself, but I am emotionally present and available for those who need my help or guidance, for anything.

More often than not I am awake until the early morning hours working on someone else's beautiful dream, and in that moment lies my sacred purpose, my IKIGAI.

those awkward moments
when I spare feelings of others
I weep while they smile

In the dance of delicate emotions,
where my silence shields their hearts,
I shed tears unseen,
hidden behind a mask of smiles.

Treasure every moment they grace with their presence, for each moment of life is unique.

Discovering your own Ikigai means to embrace your passion, mission, vocation and profession.

Ikigai is a way of life, a state of mind

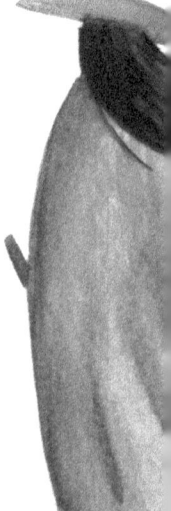

embrace your passion
vocation and profession
accept mindfulness

Make a difference in the world, one day at a time.
Find your purpose, understand what it is that makes your soul happy and truly content.

our emotions are tightly woven between all our thoughts...

finding your
IKIGAI
WORKBOOK

- What you love
- passion
- mission
- Your strengths
- IKIGAI
- The world
- profession
- vocation
- What you can be paid for

What is Ikigai?

Ikigai, which translates to "cause for existence," is a Japanese concept. Japanese words for "life" and "value" are "iki" and "gai," respectively. Your ikigai is your true self, your happiness. It's what makes you happy and motivates you to get out of bed each morning.

It's crucial to note that while traditional Japanese philosophy places emphasis on discovering inner bliss, western interpretation has exploited ikigai as a means of locating your dream job.

According to the Westernized form of ikigai, you've found your dream job if it has the following four characteristics:

- a thing you love
- What the world needs
- what you're good at and
- what you can charge for.

The four primary overlapping qualities in this ikigai diagram help you visualise this idea:

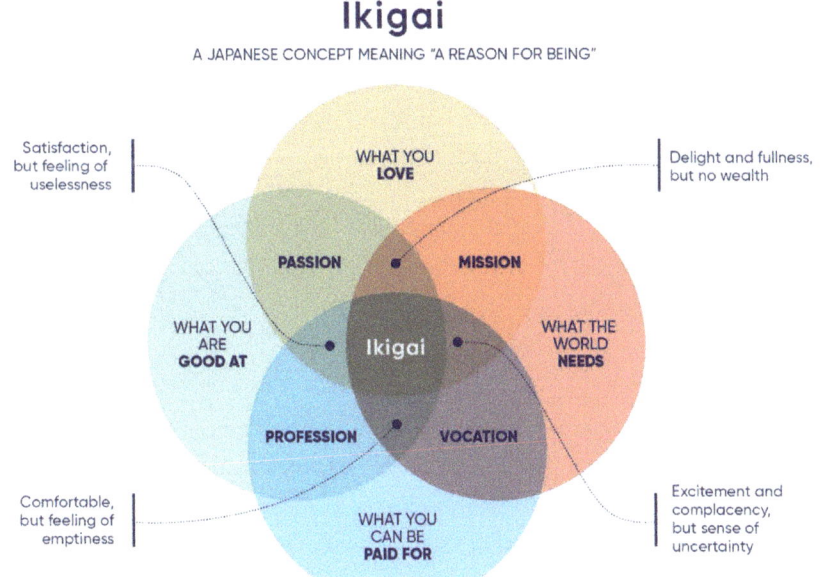

Ikigai

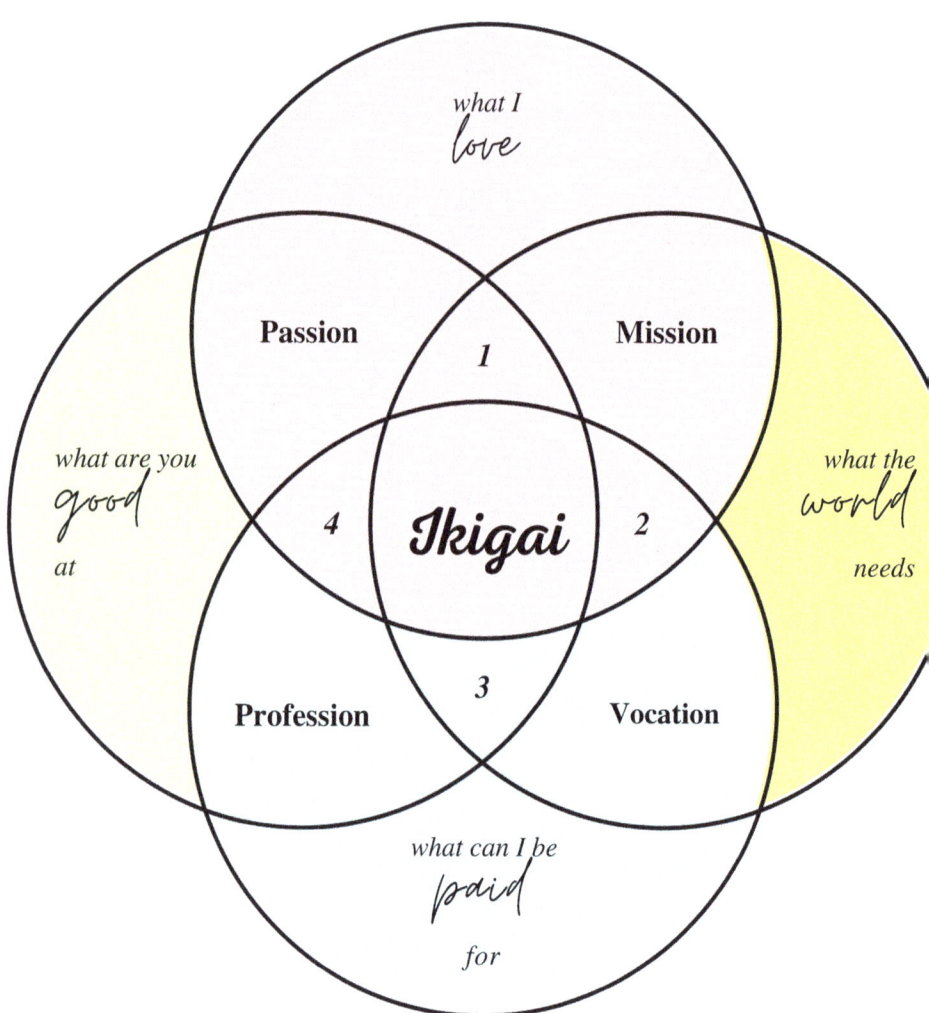

1. True happiness, but little to no financial security.
2. Excitement and enthusiasm, but a sense of uncertainty.
3. Satisfied but a feeling of emptiness from a lack of meaning in life.
4. Financially comfortable & generally satisfied, but a feeling of uselessness.

How to find your Ikigai?

- RECOGNIZE WHAT IKIGAI IMPLIES
- COMPLETE YOUR IKIGAI CHART.
- IDENTIFY OVERLAPPING ANSWERS
- FIND YOUR IKIGAI'S MISSING CIRCLE OR CIRCLES.
- DISCUSS ABOUT THE MISSING CIRCLE (S)

Getting Ready for your Ikigai

Tamashiro (2019) emphasises that the person needs to get ready ikigai.

end some time thinking about the following to set the stage for the xt adjustments (Tamashiro, 2019):

1. Always remember that you are what you do, not who you are at work.
2. Don't take pleasure lightly.
3. Find activities you like. You will look for others after carrying them out.

DISCOVERING YOUR
Ikigai

Below there are a set of questions/journal prompts, that you may fill up to answer the important Ikigai questions (a thing you love, What the world needs, what you're good at and what you can charge for).

At the end of the section, there will be a keyword prompt, where you can fill up the keywords from that particular section & fill it up in your Ikigai Chart.

What do you love?

You should choose an enjoyable activity for your ikigai. Any activity that makes you feel good and that you would undertake voluntarily at any moment can qualify. Your dopamine levels will rise as a result of it, and you would jump at the chance to discuss it and spread the word about it to others whenever the opportunity presents itself. It might be as simple as engaging in a pastime that you truly enjoy, such as writing, making movies, taking pictures, dancing, painting, or even collecting stamps.

A passion within my hands,
crafting my dreams with my heart
and soul daily,
stepping through my path of joy

What do you never get bored with?

When do you feel most joyful?

Do you look forward to leaving work more than you do to starting it?

Do you have a passion for a certain pastime or craft?

Even if you were not paid, what work would you continue to do?

Are you emotionally invested in your pastime or profession?

When did you last lose track of time? What were you doing?

Imagine your dream profession, what are the things you love the most about it?

Keywords from this section

Revisit your prompts from this section, & make a note of the words/actions that are repeated the most (this will help you later on, in filling up the Ikigai Chart).

What are you GOOD *at?*

Finding out what you are or would like to be good at might also help you come closer discovering your ikigai. Is there anything you're naturally good at? Something that yo are regarded an expert at or can do with ease? Or perhaps there is something you wan to learn how to do, something you have tried to learn how to do, or something you ha worked incredibly hard to achieve?

You might have spent years honing a skill like videography, public speaking, fashio design, marketing, counseling, or computer programming. You can now cross two tas off your list to discover your ikigai if you are doing something you enjoy and are goo at.

My ink flow daily
silent wings soaring to new heights
my story be heard

Do others approach you for advice on matters pertaining to your job or hobb[y]

Do you have any aspects of your profession or interest that come naturally to you?

Are you among the top in your field?

Are you or do you aspire to be an authority in your field?

What do you believe to be your strongest suit?

Keywords from this section

Revisit your prompts from this section, & make a note of the words/actions that are repeated the most (this will help you later on, in filling up the Ikigai Chart).

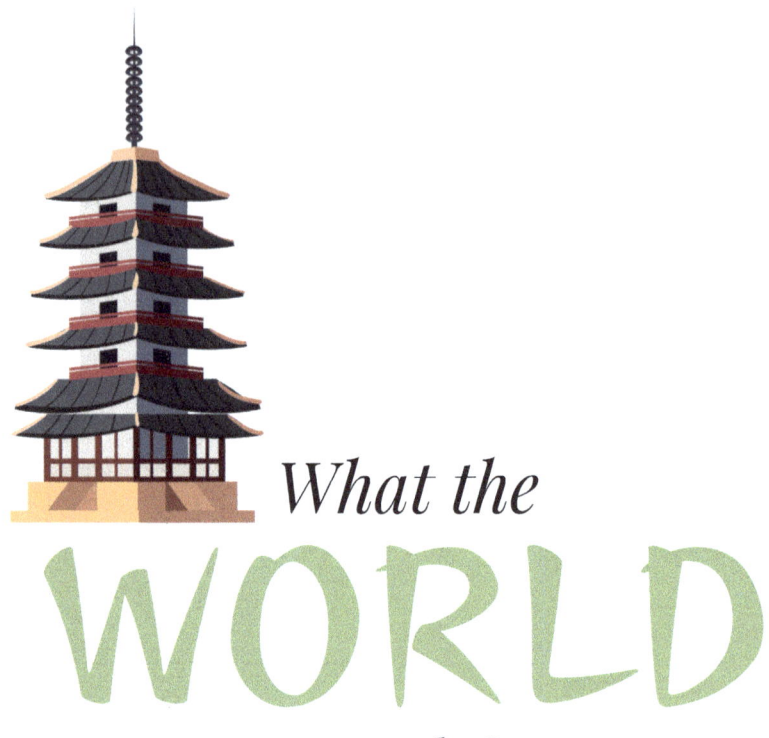

What the WORLD *needs?*

The third element is something that the globe or a society needs to find its ikigai. W feel better when we realize that what we do improves the world in which we live. W get the impression that we are contributing significantly to our neighborhood. Nowadays, a large portion of people struggle to find fulfillment in their work since th frequently fail to see its significance. Knowing that your work has the potential to impact other people's lives will help you locate your ikigai.

In each new line,
a new journey,
a new dream

Is there a significant market demand for your work?

ure the next year, 10 years, and 100 years — will your work still be of importance?

What can you do or provide that would make others' lives more meaningful?

What social issues would you like to contribute to resolving?

What is missing from the world?

How could you become more active in your neighborhood?

Keywords from this section

Revisit your prompts from this section, & make a note of the words/actions that are repeated the most (this will help you later on, in filling up the Ikigai Chart).

What can you be PAID for?

Knowing what you can be rewarded for might help you identify your ikigai. Keep in mind that in order to support our requirements and expenses on a daily basis, we need to make money. So, ideally, your ikigai should be something that can earn you money. Simply enjoying your work and being skilled at it are insufficient. It's important that you receive fair payment for it and that it enables you to put food on the table and clothing on your back.

My words
spreading daily,
hopefully to inspire
more dreaming poets.

Does anyone else receive payment for the same work that you do?

Do you or will you eventually be able to support yourself well through your work?

Is the degree of competition for your job healthy?

If you weren't working at your current job, what would you be doing

Which roles, responsibilities, or jobs catch your attention?

Do you currently earn a good livelihood in your profession?

Keywords from this section

Revisit your prompts from this section, & make a note of the words/actions that are repeated the most (this will help you later on, in filling up the Ikigai Chart).

FILLING UP YOUR

Ikigai

Collect the keywords from the four main question sections from above, & start filling up your ikigai chart.

If you're feeling overwhelmed by the amount of information you gathered, use the very first page following this to narrow your keywords down.

Let's narrow it down.

Love

Good

World

Paid

Ikigai

fill this up (fill only love, world, paid & good here)

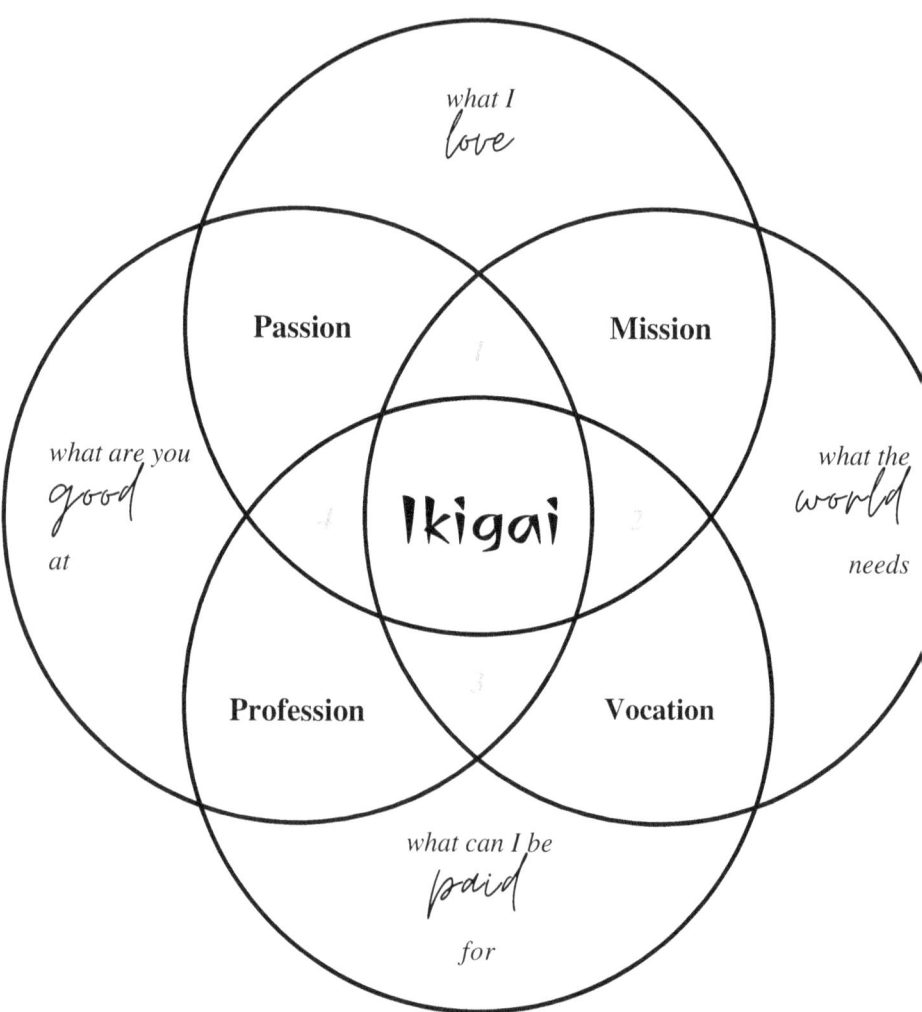

1. True happiness, but little to no financial security.
2. Excitement and enthusiasm, but a sense of uncertainty.
3. Satisfied but a feeling of emptiness from a lack of meaning in life.
4. Financially comfortable & generally satisfied, but a feeling of uselessness.

UNDERSTANDING YOUR

Ikigai

Refer to the above Ikigai chart (post-filling) then write down the passion, mission, vocation & profession parts (from overlapping parts of each intersecting circles) to understand them and figure them out.

PASSION

You've found your passion if it's something you enjoy doing and are good [at]. Unfortunately, some people who follow their passion experience happine[ss] and contentment. However, some of them might think that their work is n[ot] having much of an influence or providing them with any real benefits.

If you find yourself in a similar scenario, you may want to consider how yo[ur] enthusiasm can catch on, attract people's attention, and ultimately alter the[ir] life. Additionally, if you can figure out a means to make money from yo[ur] interest, that will allow you to complete four of the four goals to achieve ikiga[i].

For instance, if you love gardening and are an expert at growing plan[ts,] designing gardens, and even transforming a desolate area of land into [a] sanctuary of greenery, you might want to use that skill to start a small far[m] that you can use to make money.

You can raise a variety of decorative plants and flowers and then sell them [to] your neighborhood's residents. You can begin posting images of your plan[ts] online, create an online brand for your small farm, and join communities [of] gardening and farming aficionados to expand your market.

PASSION

find out your passion (love + good)

MISSION

Someone with a mission is someone who has something they enjoy that a[lso] fills a need in the world. People who are on a mission frequently beco[me] ardent supporters of their causes. Another possibility is that they are [a] humanitarian striving to make a difference in the world by participating [in] volunteer projects or providing free services to those in need. Having t[he] knowledge that you are changing the world can make you feel fulfilled, but y[ou] might not be getting paid fairly for what you are doing.

If this applies to you, you may be one of those people who hasn't yet work[ed] out how to better your craft and effectively sell your skills. Because you ne[ed] more than just desire to be regarded as an expert in a particular industry. [To] support what you love and believe in, you will also need to have sho[wn] expertise and skills. This may also be the cause of your continued lack [of] financial success despite your commitment to your objective.

You might begin by training in order to discover your ikigai. To excel at wh[at] you love, get a formal degree. Given that it is already making a difference in t[he] community, all it will take is a little time to hone your skills and eventua[lly] increase your potential to become not only an advocate but also an author[ity] in your industry.

As you gain expertise in your profession, you may utilize your newly gain[ed] abilities and knowledge to negotiate pay and begin making a living doing wh[at] you love while also making a difference in the world.

MISSION

find out your mission (love + world)

VOCATION

You have now discovered your calling if you have something that the world needs and are paid for it. Some people who are pursuing careers are occasionally unsatisfied with what they do. Additionally, not all of them are necessarily highly knowledgeable or consistently regarded as experts in their fields.

If you believe that you fall into this category, you'll need to learn how to improve your skills and make your job something you enjoy. You might be able by perhaps obtaining a degree or by enrolling in training sessions that will help you hone your talents if you want to transform your profession into your ikigai.

Additionally, you can seek to advance your professional experience and ultimately master your field.
Your work will ultimately become more enjoyable once you have made it something you can do extremely well, and you will start to see it as your newfound ikigai.

VOCATION

find out your vocation (paid + world)

PROFESSION

You have a profession if you're one of the many people who do something w[ell] enough to be compensated for it. You might be making a good living a[s a] professional doing something you've pretty much perfected. You are typica[lly] compensated highly since people like you are regarded as authorities in yo[ur] profession.

However, earning money for what you do well does not necessarily transl[ate] into doing what you love and changing the world. If you are at a stage in yo[ur] life when you have been working really hard but do not feel fulfilled, you m[ay] need to modify the way you live your life.

You might want to consider how your profession might assist you identify wh[at] you enjoy doing and learn how it can make a difference in the world in order [to] discover your ikigai.

For instance, if you are a seasoned financial expert with a strong professio[nal] network in your field and a solid reputation, you can use your network [to] launch a charity or to raise money for the less fortunate. You can also instru[ct] less privileged people who want to follow in your footsteps as a well-kno[wn] expert in your industry by using your understanding of the financial world [to] provide free coaching to small businesses or even to do so. In this manner, y[ou] are making a good difference in the lives of others. You may feel more fulfill[ed] and begin to enjoy what you do as a result of the difference you are making.

PROFESSION

find out your profession (paid + good)

Keywords/Key actions that can be derivated from this section

Passion

Mission

Profession

Vocation

FINDING YOUR
Ikigai

fill the below Ikigai chart up with references from section 2 & 3

Ikigai

fill this up (fill all)

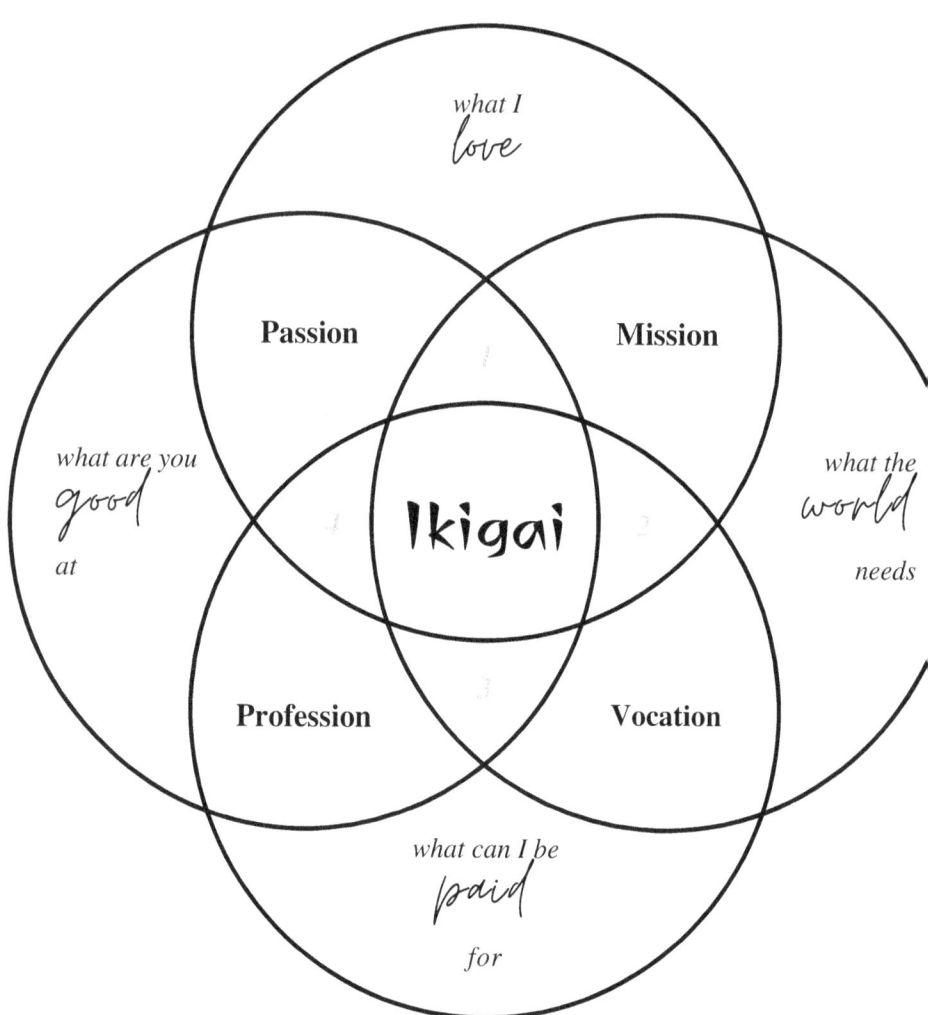

1. True happiness, but little to no financial security.
2. Excitement and enthusiasm, but a sense of uncertainty.
3. Satisfied but a feeling of emptiness from a lack of meaning in life.
4. Financially comfortable & generally satisfied, but a feeling of uselessness.

Ikigai

find the overlapping portion, in the above chart, & that's your ikigai!

you wish, go ahead and write a prompt about it, what you deciphered, how it feels, what are your thoughts on this, etc.

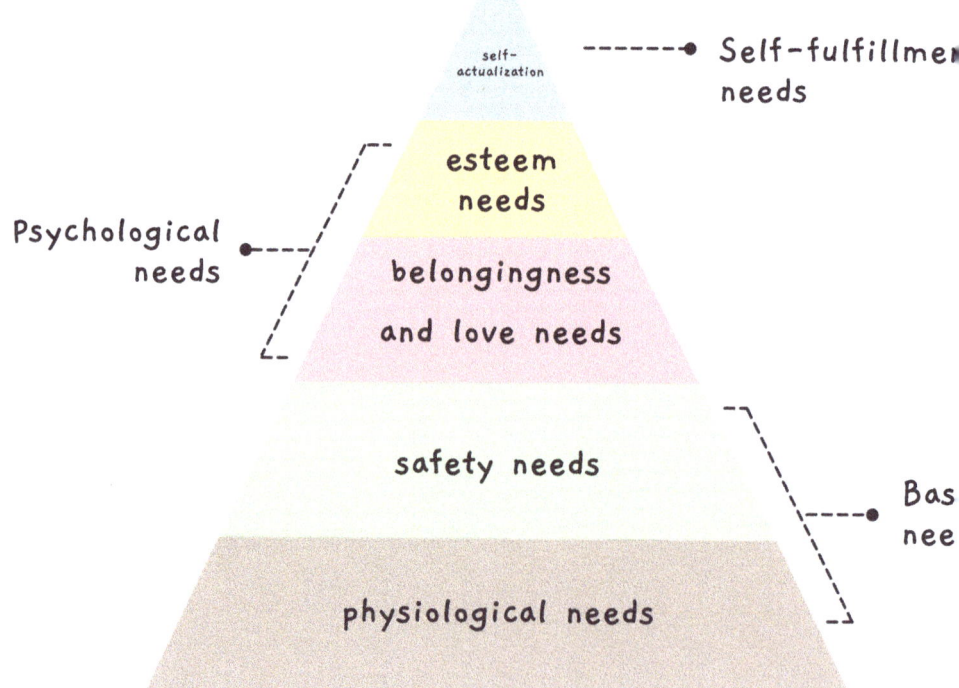

CREATE A VISUAL

Following the completion of the questions, you will begin to notice the themes and keywords that you will utilise to construct your Ikigai map. As you jot things down, check in with your thoughts and feelings. Are you feeling happy? scared*? worried to death?

In addition, feeling frightened is okay. It can be an indication that you are about to take on a bigger role. Avoid allowing fear to hold you back. In this article about identifying your blockages, we go into further detail on that.

Consider your mission, vocation, passion, and profession as potential points of intersection for each of these areas as a next step. Although it's an optional step, it might assist you in developing a list of possibilities that are a little more focused.

BRAINSTORMING

Spend some time imagining your perfect day from beginning to end. Unbelievable as it may seem, this will assist you in discovering your ikigai and actual purpose.

- What do you have on?
- To whom are you speaking?
- What do you have to say?
- Pay close attention to your feelings. What about your job gives you joy?

Make sure to write it down when you're done envisioning (or write it down as you're visualising).

Examine the inquiries to which you responded "no" next.
Spend some time coming up with tiny adjustments you can make to better align your mission.
Consider how this relates to what you enjoy doing, what you are good at, what the world needs, and how much money you can make.

Did you, for instance, respond "no" to the question, "Do you have an emotional connection to your job results?"
Perhaps you prefer to interact with clients in person rather than over the phone, or perhaps you want to apply for a leadership promotion at work.

If you said "no" to the question "Does your hobby or craft feel intuitive?"
Perhaps you should enrol in some classes to improve your abilities and make your work seem more natural.

Make locating your core, or ikigai, the main focus of your efforts during this procedure.

Note: It's common for uncertainty, worry, or bad ideas to surface at this time.
It can be difficult to face the future.
The key is to avoid giving meaning to your uncertainties and anxieties.

BRAINSTORMING
create the visuals here

STUDYING

You can now visualise how your ideal workday would appear in your he Consider studying, doing research, enrolling in classes, or getting a coach mentor right now. You can determine if your vision aligns with y expectations for the real world at this step.

Consider the possibility that you wish to photograph weddings.
But you realise it's not for you after getting some coaching from a seasor wedding photographer.

Or perhaps you wanted to sell antique clothing but after learning more ab the procedure decided you didn't want to manage such a large inventory.

Congratulations, it appears that you have identified your ikigai if you go throu this process and discover that your vision matches your expectations for yo real-life experience.
See how to say it in the following section.

If the contrary is true, relax; finding your ikigai may take some time.

Until you discover your ikigai, repeat steps one through three with a differe profession, pastime, or trade. If you're still having trouble finding it, think ab exploring and dabbling in different professions or crafts.

It doesn't matter if you bake cakes, learn to code, volunteer, start a reading cl or create a logo. Try new things until you discover something that calls to you

Not all aspects of your job must be enjoyable for you to have found yo ikigai. It indicates that you are ready to embrace everything, even t flaws. Your career is in line with what you enjoy, what you are paid fo and what the world needs, so this is why.

STUDYING

create the visuals here

IMPLEMENTING YOUR
IKIGAI

Please stick with me since this final step may be the most crucial one. It's about incorporating everything into your life. Ikigai manifests in a variety of ways, and this is how you discover your purpose: by fusing a number of enjoyable and fulfilling pursuits.

This part is divided into 4 parts.

THE FOUR STEPS TO IMPLEMENT YOUR IKIGAI

STEP 1

Set small goals

STEP 2

Make a plan

STEP 3

Establish a support system

STEP 4

Try it out

Step 1: Create Small Goals.

Use the ideas you've come up with for potential solutions to establish specific annual goals. Create manageable monthly goals to aid in achieving your annual goals after you've written them down. The secret is to make small, incremental progress toward your long-term objective.

Step 2: Plan it out!

Create weekly (or even daily) goals using your monthly goals as a guide.

Organize your list of long-term and short-term objectives now that you have it.

Include rituals, hobbies, jobs, roles & relationships.

Step 3: Create a support system

A support network is essential for discovering your mission.

Contact mentors, coaches, instructors, and other experts who have accomplished comparable feats to build a support network. You can join forces with those who share your objectives by locking arms.

Develop your network of contacts and learn all you can from those who are in your corner.

Step 4: Testing

It's time to put your official plan to the test now that it's ready to go. Are your immediate and long-term objectives being met? What's bothering you, exactly? What is happening?

Currently, are you able to say "yes" to every inquiry from step 1? If not, you might want to review your plans and goals. Is my attention focused on what I ought to do or what I want to do at this point?

Enable your Ikigai to Flourish.

(Ken Mogi, author of "The little book of Ikigai", highlights five pillars that will help you uncover your sources of Ikigai and clarify your purpose.)

1. Take small steps.
2. Accept yourself & your uniqueness.
3. Be mindful of the impact your actions may have on others & the environment you live in.
4. Create a daily routine.
5. Focus on the present.

4 steps of finding your *ikigai*

Find your own purpose

1. Find your own purpose

2. Learn as much as you want

3. Find your support system

4. It is okay to fall and hit reset

RANK YOUR PRIORITIES IN LIFE FROM TOP TO BOTTOM

- love
- family
- friends
- passion
- success
- wellness

www.ingramcontent.com/pod-product-compliance
Lightning Source LLC
Chambersburg PA
CBHW062053290426
44109CB00027B/2813